STAND UP PADDLEBOARDING

A BEGINNER'S GUIDE

SIMON BASSETT

FERNHURST

BOOKS

A catalogue record for this book is available from the British Library
ISBN 978-1-912177-97-4

Fernhurst Books and Simon Bassett would like to thank Holly Bassett for participating in the photoshoot, Tim Hore for taking the photos and David Williams for providing and driving the RIB and the Jeep.

All photographs by Tim Hore © Fernhurst Books except:
Front cover, p2, 4, 5, 34 (top), 35 (top right), 36, 40, 41, 44, 45: © 2XS ®: Sandy Clunas, Simon Bassett, Holly Basset, Jake Sparks
Back cover, p35 (bottom), 38, 42, 43 © Fanatic: Klaas Voget, Sebastian Schoeffel, Michael Kalensky, Aurelian le Metaier, Max Prechtel
p34 (bottom) © Dave White/SUP Armada
p39 © Si Crother/APP

Designed & illustrated by Daniel Stephen
Printed in the UK by Latimer Trend

CONTENTS

INTRODUCTION

Stand Up Paddleboarding (SUP) is a relatively new watersport. In the last 10 years it has exploded worldwide. Its growth has been driven by its accessibility to so many stretches of water from inland rivers, lakes and canals to coastal estuaries and surf locations.

SUP has transcended other watersports because it is so diverse: you can paddle on flat water, surf, tour, race, join a club or take a holiday with your SUP. You can also use SUP for fitness or yoga.

You can buy a board for every option in epoxy from 7ft (210cm) to 18ft (550cm). You can use one of many different models of inflatable board, pump it up, ride it and then pack it away into the size of large backpack and stick it into the boot of your car. You can take your dog out on a SUP, go fishing, ride white-water and even take the whole family on a Mega SUP.

My journey into SUP started in 2006 after hearing about Laird Hamilton crossing the English Channel on a new type of surfboard craft with a single-bladed paddle. Timo Mullen called me and said, "Let's buy some boards!"

I started to SUP on a tandem Surftech surfboard with paddles imported from Hawaii. At the time we were part of very small group of paddleboarders – there were less than 10 in the UK. They were exciting times, lots of things happened very quickly. By 2007, the British Stand Up Paddle Association (BSUPA) had been set up after the first UK SUP contest in Watergate Bay. By 2008, Andy Gratwick and I had started developing the BSUPA teaching scheme and I had also run, with others, the first BSUPA National SUP series.

I hope this SUP Beginner's Guide will help provide some basic knowledge, advice, technical tips and water safety to start you on a lifelong journey on the water with your SUP.

Simon Bassett

PADDLE, BOARD, LEASH

PADDLE

Adjust your paddle before you head out to around 6 inches (15cm) taller than yourself. Take a look at the diagram, which gives a guide to all terminology and how and where everything fits.

Handle

Adjustment mechanism

Shaft

Paddle neck

Blade /paddle head

Blade width in inches /cm

Front face

Back face

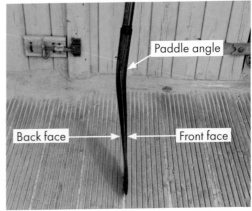

Paddle angle

Back face

Front face

BOARD

Volume is the board's total cubic measurement – measured in litres – which supports your body weight.

When you place your board on any hard surface, such as land, the hull can dent or get damaged if there are sharp stones. Also take care with fins as these are prone to break.

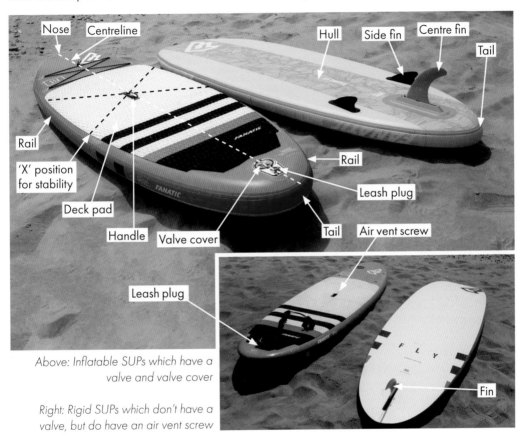

Above: Inflatable SUPs which have a valve and valve cover

Right: Rigid SUPs which don't have a valve, but do have an air vent screw

LEASH

Your leash should be the same length as your board. Coiled for flat water, straight for surf.

Attach the leash to the board before carrying it, and to yourself at the water's edge – the leash should be attached to your back leg. (Whichever foot you would naturally use to kick a football should be your front, or lead, foot so you put your leash on the other leg.)

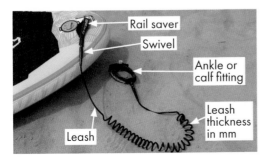

PADDLE GEAR

There is a vast array of water wear you can buy: your local SUP shop should be a help.

WETSUITS

Wetsuits suitable for the season is the general rule because hypothermia and cold-water shock are realities without the correct gear on the water. You can always peel down your suit if you get hot, rather than getting cold and wishing you had worn one out on the water.

A 5/4mm wetsuit thickness is ideal in winter and 3/2mm in summer. Most decent wetsuits are blind stitched and glued, so the seams don't let water in or out and are flexible.

Summer (left) & winter (right) wetsuits

It is hard to tell the difference visually, but their thickness is marked

HANDS, FEET & HEAD

Booties and wet shoes are ideal for grip and keeping your feet from minor cuts and scratches; gloves and headwear depend on how cool or hot it is.

BUOYANCY AIDS

Buoyancy aids are an essential piece of gear to begin with, adding some warmth but, more importantly, giving floatation. Each buoyancy aid should have a CE mark with a weight guide. When you try on a buoyancy aid it needs to fit securely round your chest and not be loose on the shoulders. A flatter profile buoyancy aid is ideally suited to SUP as it makes it easier to get back on the board from the water.

The complete kit

A good fitting buoyancy aid

PERSONAL BELONGINGS

A waterproof bag is a good way to store your phone, car keys, spares and supplies. There are quite a few options including bum bags, phone-only bags, backpacks or dry wet bags. It is always best to store your main kit (i.e. phone) on your body rather than in a dry bag attached to the board.

CE mark and weight guide on a buoyancy aid

Waterproof backpacks

LAUNCH, PRONE, KNEEL, STAND, PADDLE

LAUNCH

Heading out for the first time, carry your board safely towards the water's edge holding the leash and then attach the leash to your back leg (see page 7). Avoid walking on land wearing your leash.

Carry the board holding the leash

Attach the leash at the water's edge

Grab the board's handle in, let's say, your left hand, hold the paddle in the right and walk into the water until it's waist-deep.

Think about the wind direction. It is always best to enter the water with the board on your leeward side (downwind side of you) – if you have to let it go, the board will drift away from your body.

The ideal SUP conditions are a gentle onshore wind (under 10 knots, but closer to 0 knots is

best), ankle-height chop or less, with no current or water flow. Always try to place your board directly into the wind so a gust cannot flip it over.

PRONE

Climb onto the board then lie down on it with the paddle tucked under your chest (prone position) and your chest around the handle area. Then paddle out with your hands like a surfer, and practise turning around using your hands to steer. Think about your body position on the board and keep the board flat on the water surface – trim the board slightly by moving forward or back.

Paddling in prone position

KNEEL

Check the water is deep enough – waist-deep or more – and kneel down on the board over the board handle. Hold the paddle, knuckles facing forward, hands shoulder-width apart and bottom hand close to the paddle blade / head.

From the prone position

Raise your torso

Get onto your knees

Move your knees forward

Get up to kneeling

And start paddling

Paddle three strokes on each side, reaching as far forward as you can to initiate the stroke, and releasing the paddle from the water in front of your knees. This gives a short paddle stroke.

Paddle from forward   *To in front of your knees*   *Paddle both sides*

Practise turning by pushing the water under the nose of the board with the front face of the paddle.

Push the water   *Under the nose*

Push the water under the nose again   *Until you have turned*

STAND

Check the water is deep enough (waist-deep or more) – use your paddle as a depth finder. Position your board into the wind and waves before you stand up. From a kneeling position move so that your feet are parallel either side of the board handle, hands out in front with the paddle across the deck at 90° with one hand over the paddle handle and the other holding the shaft of the paddle.

Slowly stand up using the paddle as a third leg. Put pressure on the paddle blade and, keeping the blade in the water, come up to a standing position, flexed knees, torso upright, eyes on the horizon and feet shoulder-width apart. To keep stability, you need to be on the move – start the short paddle stroke as soon as you can.

Get onto your front foot

Then your back foot

And stand up

Using the paddle as a third leg

Till upright

And then start paddling

STANCE

How you stand on your SUP will affect your balance and the trim of the board. Most SUPs have the handle positioned at the point of balance on the centreline of the board. You place your feet in a parallel stance either side of the handle, shoulder-width apart. Soften your knees, keep your torso upright, eyes on the horizon and head position upright (not leaning forward).

To help your balance: look where you're going (horizon), not at the front of the board; your knees absorb the chop and help keep your balance. Keeping your torso upright is key to setting your balance and not bending at your hips.

The core is often talked about here to help with your stability on the board: try sucking your belly button slightly towards your spine and lift upwards – this will assist with your balance and help keep you using the right muscle groups while you paddle. The core is the fine mesh of muscles that connect the torso to the legs and sit under your abdominals – as you get older this muscle deactivates, so in SUP it's key to reactivate this muscle as it helps your ability to balance and ensures you have good posture.

FALLING SAFELY

Well, it's just going to happen: we all fall off our paddleboards and most of the time there are no issues. However, there are a few things to be aware of. Never dive off your SUP as you do not know the water depth. If you are falling, try to fall away from the board flat and try to keep the paddle above your head so you don't land on or break your paddle. Hold the paddle above your head, ideally gripping the paddle with both hands.

The correct stance: feet parallel either side of the handle, shoulder-width apart, soft knees, torso upright, eyes on the horizon

If you are falling

Hold the paddle above your head

And fall away from the board

Falling flat

RECOVERY STROKE

When you are up and paddling and lose your balance, the recovery stroke is a great way to regain your balance and not fall in. You effectively use your paddle as a brace or third leg. You can use the paddle slap recovery stroke at any time: when turning, paddling along and when you get in wavy or surf-type conditions.

So, if your feet are in a parallel stance and you start losing your balance, go quickly into squat, crouch down and use the front face of your paddle to slap the water. Position the paddle in front of your body at a 75° angle, extend your arms forward and feel the pressure from the blade head as it makes contact with the water. As soon as you regain your stability, return to a more upright stance and carry on paddling.

This stroke will save loads of energy compared to climbing on the board each time you fall.

Crouch and slap the water

Use the paddle as support

And return to standing

15

SHORT PADDLE STROKE

The short paddle stroke is the result of a combination of your stance, body position on the board and inertia of your paddle – together this drives and helps steer the board in one smooth movement. Like many things it takes time to perfect.

To start, set your feet either side of the handle on your SUP a shoulder-width apart – keep your feet parallel and position them to trim your board so it sits flat on the water. Keep your head and eyes on the horizon, shoulders over the middle of your feet, soft knees and keep your torso upright (see page 14).

Your paddle should have been adjusted on land so it's roughly 6 inches (15cm) taller than you.

To start the stroke, place your hands on the paddle, shoulder-width apart, with your top arm gripping the handle with an overhand grip and with your blade hand gripping the shaft of the paddle tightly.

Keep your arms fairly straight and rotate slightly from the hips when you paddle. Now reach forward with the paddle and place the paddle parallel to the rail on one side of the board (Catch).

Place the tip of the paddle in the water and bend your knees: compress so the paddle is in the water up to its neck. Then, in one smooth movement, pull the water towards your body (Pull). Push with your top hand to drive the paddle. Try to keep the paddle vertical so it keeps the board moving in a straight line.

When used correctly, the paddle acts like a counter balance throughout the stroke and, while you are paddling, it provides extra stability like a third leg.

To release the paddle from the water, drop the top hand across the board (from 12 to 3 o'clock) while holding the paddle, the blade should exit the water in front of your feet. Once the paddle exits the water, swap hands – the top hand to bottom hand and start paddling on the opposite side.

Key points to remember:
* 3 strokes either side
* Keep the stroke short
* Keep your eyes on the horizon
* Try to keep the paddle vertical
* Exit the paddle from water in front of feet

Changing sides: Release the paddle by dropping the top hand, changing hands and paddling on the other side

Put the blade in the water (catch)

Pull the water towards you (pull)

Till the paddle is in front of your feet

Release the paddle out of the water

From the correct stance

Reach forward with the paddle

VERTICAL PADDLE STROKE

There are lots of elements of the paddle stroke that need to come together to get a smooth efficient stroke and this will take some practice. To stop the row effect (causing your board to turn) and keep your board in a straight line it's important to understand the vertical part of your paddle stoke.

Your top hand (handle) needs to be over the edge of the board rail when you paddle with your lower hand (nearest the blade) directly underneath your top hand when it's in its vertical position.

As you paddle, arch your body to get your top hand over the rail. If your paddle is on the right-hand side of the board, your hips arch to the left – this helps keep the paddle vertical and reduces the row effect. Arch your hips to the right if the paddle is on the left-hand side of the board.

You can also assist this by keeping the paddle stroke short and reducing the amount of water you are pulling. Keeping a higher cadence stroke, pulling less water, will give less fatigue and more speed for less effort.

When you practise this, try doing a very slow pace: don't rush so you can figure out how this works for you.

Try to get the paddle vertical

Arch so the paddle is vertical

Keep hand over hand as you pull the water

Which will keep the board in a straight line

STEERING WITH YOUR PADDLE & FEET

The row effect on a SUP is the effect of the force of the paddle pulling water along the rail (trying to turn the board) versus the fin / fins trying to keep the board in a straight line. So, for example, if you paddle on the right, the board turns to the left.

A short paddle stroke is one of the key elements in reducing this and long gondola-type paddle strokes will not help keep your board in a straight line.

Start by making sure your paddle is vertical against the rail of the board, hands are over each other and your paddle blade is angled (see photo) so it helps redirect the water slightly under the board.

Your paddle stroke also needs to be smooth through the pull section of the stroke; keep the blade in the water, at least up to the neck, so you get maximum force from the stroke. Your compression and body release in the stroke help get the drive out of your paddle action.

In addition, as you paddle on the right-hand side of the board, add some weight to the right-hand rail. Once you switch paddle sides to the left side, add weight to left rail and this will help maintain a straight line.

Key points to remember:
- Short paddle stroke
- Vertical paddle
- If it's windy you might paddle more on the windward side (the rail the wind is blowing onto): say 3 to 1
- Keep an eye on your distance from the shore
- Keep your head up and keep your eyes on the horizon, not looking at the board

Arch your hips, keep the paddle vertical against the rail of the board

Angle the paddle so it helps redirect the water slightly under the board

Exit the stroke in front of your feet

Add some weight to the rail next to the paddle

TURNING

PUSH TURN

For the Push Turn you need to think about how the water is redirected under the board. You're still in a parallel stance with your arms out in front of you. The Push Turn is simple: place the front face of the paddle in the water between the nose and front of the deck pad and push the water **underneath** the front of the board. Repeat this until the board has turned, then return to the short paddle stroke and carry on.

To alter the speed of the turn, think about the depth of the blade in the water. If less than half of the blade is in the water, you get less pressure on your arms and a slower turn. If all the blade is in the water, up to the neck, you will feel the most pressure and get a more positive turn. When you hold the paddle, you are tending to use your lower arm to push the paddle.

When you push the water under the board nose at 90° to the board, it will turn pretty much on its axis. Think of this like a bow thruster on a boat, which jets water under or away from the hull to adjust the direction of the craft.

Push the water underneath the front of the board in a series of strokes to turn the board

SWEEP TURN

The Sweep Turn is effectively doing the opposite to the Push Turn – you're pushing water **away** from the nose at 90° to the board rather than pushing it underneath the board.

Again, start in a parallel stance. Keep your arms extended out in front of your body, with the paddle between the nose and front of the deck pad. Then place the paddle in the water and use the back face of the paddle to push the water at 90° away from the board.

Push the water away from the board in a series of strokes to turn the board

When you are doing these turns use a short paddle stroke and you can either use half or the whole blade in the water to make the turn. There is no real need to do this fast, but the key is the 90° to get the best result out of your turn. Don't forget: if you lose your balance, use the recovery stroke!

STEP BACK TURN

The Step Back or Pivot Turn is great way to change the direction of the board or complete a full 180° turn without losing momentum. It requires good balance and paddle skills to turn quickly but can be learnt by a beginner in flat water.

In this turn we are going to change from a parallel stance to your leash foot moving further back on the board. The idea of this turn is that you should be able turn the board on its axis and within the length of the board.

We are starting this turn at the basic level, so we start with parallel feet either side of the handle. Keep your body position upright, soften your knees, eyes on the horizon. Shift your leash foot towards the rear of the board but you don't need to move it far, a maximum of maybe 12 inches (30cm). Place this back foot across the board with the toes and heel facing either rail. Keep your knees flexed and think about the 'X' position of your feet diagonal – avoid standing along the centreline.

If your leash, for example, is on your left foot,

From the correct stance

Move your leash foot back with your feet diagonal

Release and return your paddle

To the rail

this will become your back foot in the turn and you paddle on the left side of the board pulling from the nose on that side.

Use your paddle in similar way to the Sweep Turn, where it is positioned in the water between the nose and front of the deck pad, and pull the water in short arcs away from the board at 90° to the board. Remember in this turn to use the recovery stroke if you lose your balance: it's a great way not to fall in.

The key part of this turn is to angle the paddle and push the water away from the board at 90° – keep the stroke short, the paddle at blade depth during the turn, feet positioned either side of the 'X'. To help the board turn faster you can add some weight to your rear foot (the one nearest back of the board).

As you improve, try the turn the other way by moving your opposite (non-leash) foot to the back of the board and repeating the whole turn. This will give you greater manoeuvrability on the water, allowing you to turn both ways.

Push the water away 90° from the rail

Keep the strokes short

And push the water again

90° away from the rail until turned

REVERSE PADDLE TURN

The Reverse Paddle Turn is a good one to use if you want to change direction fast. It is an ideal turn for manoeuvring around other paddleboarders and fixed objects in the water but, because of the twist in your back as you turn, it's worth being warmed up before attempting it.

This turn is generally done as you are slowing down or stationary.

Start with your feet in a parallel stance and think about your stance and head position – eyes on the horizon.

Hold the paddle out in front of your body and, if you are going to turn to the right, the paddle starts with the blade pointing towards the left. Hold the paddle with your right hand over the handle. Keep the paddle at 90° degrees across the board with the front face of the paddle facing the front of the board. Take a look at the picture of this, it can be confusing!

If we turn to the right, the paddle swings over the nose of the board to the opposite side, so in this case: left to right. Place the blade in the water on the right and use the back face of the paddle to push the water under the board.

Keep the paddle handle at hip height to help with your balance and think about how much pressure you want from the paddle by either using half or the whole blade up to the neck for maximum force in the turn.

The paddle still remains fairly vertical. Spread your hands at shoulder width and flex your knees. Once the board has turned, start your short paddle stroke.

To add some control and increase the accuracy of the turn, if your paddle is on the right side of the board put more pressure on the right foot and do the opposite when your paddle is on the left-hand side of your board.

You can use part of the reverse paddle turn to change direction slightly or to manoeuvre around objects. It's certainly worth practising this, as you get more confident on your SUP.

From paddling on the left

Pull the paddle towards the board

To the other side

Take the paddle over to the right

Put the paddle in the water

PULL

Pulling the water underneath the board

Release your paddle

And paddle again

To continue the turn

FORWARD STEERING TURN

This turn is about steering the board while moving forward and changing the board's direction while paddling. It might be to correct your paddling line or to avoid a fixed buoy or pass another paddleboard.

To make this turn, the board needs to be moving forward – the more board speed, the more effective this turn will become.

Let's assume we are paddling along; the paddle is entering the water on the left rail of the board and we want to turn around a fixed object in the water on the right-hand side of the board.

Firstly, keep your knees soft, slightly squat down as you do this and swing your paddle across the nose of the board. The handle of your paddle is in your right hand and your left hand is on the shaft of the paddle a shoulder-width apart.

Keep your paddle handle at hip height and place the paddle or its edge into the water with the front face of the blade pointing away from the rail and back face toward the rail.

The angle of the paddle is nearly parallel to the rail once in the water, again entering the water between the nose and front of the deck pad and you now adjust the angle to change the direction of the board. This is fairly subtle: just open the face of the paddle away from the board towards the object you want to go around, and the speed of the board will dictate the turning control.

A top tip on this turn is to keep the handle at hip height for balance; paddle on the right, pressure on the right rail. Think about the angle of the paddle blade, if it is too open it will act like a brake. You need board speed to turn in this way.

Get the board moving forward

Put the paddle in the water

Turning the board around

The more speed the more efficient the turn

Swing the paddle across the board

Adjust the paddle angle

To change the board's direction

And then swap sides with the paddle

And paddle normally

LANDING & LOADING ONTO A ROOF RACK

Coming off the water after a SUP session it's a good idea to approach the bank or shoreline kneeling on your board – falling off in shallow water is common and very avoidable.

Once you reach shallow water, slow down to avoid smashing your fins, climb off your board, grab the handle and carry your SUP onto dry land. Take the leash off your leg and coil it on the leash saver or hold the leash to prevent tripping over it. Carry the board and paddle to your vehicle.

Move from standing

To kneeling

Get off the board

Take off your leash

Pick up your board

Carry it to the car

If you've been paddling in either fresh or saltwater, wash your kit down before packing it away or, if that's not possible, do it when you get home.

DEFLATING

If you have an inflatable SUP this bit is easier: deflate the board, roll it up and put it in the back of the car (see page 33 for a fuller description).

ROOF RACK

If you have a rigid board you need to get it onto the roof rack and tie it down.

Check your rack is securely fitted to your vehicle and has the correct load rating, and that the rack spacing on the car is enough to support your board (1.5m). Have some foam pads on the rack to prevent denting the board and some decent rack straps. Avoid the ratchet lever type because you can very easily over-tension the straps which results in your board's rails / hull being damaged; also the straps are often not padded around the buckle ratchet area which can cause damage.

Loop the rack straps around the rack bar – front rack and rear rack. Place the board on the rack – with the deck of the board facing down to the roof of the car. If it's windy, this is a two-person job!

You can then bring the strap over the front of the board and loop the strap round the bar and then tighten down on the buckle. At this stage, tighten it so the board can't move but don't over tighten. Then do the same at the rear.

Once you are happy with this, finally tighten both straps up so the board is secure and complete a half hitch behind the buckle with the tail end of the strap. Check the straps are not twisted so they don't vibrate all the way on the journey home!

Buy good quality rack straps – you don't want them breaking while you have a board on the roof.

Put your paddles inside the vehicle as tying them onto the rack with your board is not ideal and can damage both board and paddle.

It's worth stopping after a short time to check the board is tight on the roof rack.

Loop the straps round the bars

Lift the board onto the rack

Position the board on the rack

Attach the front strap loosely

Attach the back strap loosely

Tighten both straps

CHOOSING A BOARD & PADDLE

BOARD

Choosing a new SUP board is quite a daunting task but here are some guidelines when you are starting out. The best advice generally comes from people who use SUPs a lot, so your local SUP school or specialist watersports shop would be an ideal place to start.

An all-round type of board is ideal: you need enough volume flotation to support your body weight (see opposite) and extra flotation to help with the glide of the board.

Each brand has a different way of approaching the board design but the dimensions and volume versus your weight will determine the board you buy. You can use an all-round board in flat water, in small waves, inland and coastal waters as they tend to be versatile and forgiving to paddle. Some brands offer fittings for storage of gear and even windsurf mast foot options.

Should you buy an inflatable or rigid board? Both work but try to get a good quality brand that has put some work into the development of the shape and construction of the board.

A rigid (left) & an inflatable (right) board

RIGID BOARDS

Have a more defined rail (edge), sit in the water because of their foam epoxy construction and are more rigid than an inflatable board. They will perform better in rougher and windier conditions and have a very positive feel. But you will need a car, roof rack and storage for a rigid board – and you will need to take more care carrying it to and from the water.

Suggested board sizing:
- 70-85kg rider: 33in wide, 10/11+ft long, 180 litres
- 85-100kg rider: 33in wide, 10/11+ft long, 220 litres

INFLATABLE BOARDS

Pretty much solve all the storage issues – they fold up into a backpack-sized bag. However, you have to pump them up each time and make sure you get full pressure. They are more susceptible to wind drift, but less prone to damage. They are ideal to take on most water types and are very portable, very durable and will glide well.

Suggested board sizing:
- 70-85kg rider: 33in wide, 10.4ft long, 285 litres
- 85-100kg rider: 34in wide, 10.8ft long, 300+ litres

Rough board volume calculator:
- Rigid board: Body weight in kilos multiplied by 2.3

- Inflatable board: Body weight in kilos multiplied by 3.4.

The board's width & length also have an effect.

PADDLES

Paddles come in lots of different options but to start with an adjustable handle is ideal – pick a small blade, either composite or plastic. (You can buy an alloy, fibreglass or carbon shaft in one, two or three pieces.)

It's better to spend a little more on the paddle, as this is what drives you along. A fibreglass or carbon type is preferable. Look for a good handle shape: a T-bar or bulb-type grip.

Suggested paddle widths:
- Child: 6.5in (16cm)
- 50 / 60kg adult: 6.75-7in (17-18cm)
- 80kg+ adult: 7-8in (18-20cm)

LEASH

As a beginner, a leash is an essential piece of gear – it keeps you attached to your flotation device (board) and stops it drifting away when you fall off. The leash needs to be good quality, well made and must be securely tied to the leash plug. The leash needs to be the same length as your board.

A coiled ankle leash is ideal for beginners as it stays on top of the board. You can get a calf- or ankle-fitting version. The straight leash is ideal for use in surf (see page 7).

INFLATING & DEFLATING A BOARD

INFLATING

Inflatable SUPs (ISUPs) need to be inflated. You get a hand-activated pump supplied with your board, with high / low pressure settings and a pressure gauge. The gauge has measurements indicated in PSI / BAR.

Roll your board out flat. (Don't worry about fitting the fin first, if you have that type.) Take the valve cover off and you will notice, when you look at the valve, that you have a centre plastic sprung nut. This valve has open and shut positions operated by turning the sprung nut to the left or right. Depress and lock the nut to deflate. To inflate, make sure the sprung nut is not depressed and turn left or right and gently push down to unlock. This is not obvious at first but, when you attach the hose from your pump, make sure that the spring-pressured centre nut is fully locked.

When inflating your board, check there is no debris / sand around the pump or valve area.

Pumps supplied by different brands have high- and low-pressure settings: a low-pressure setting to start to fill the board full of air and then a high-pressure setting to finish off, so it becomes hard and set to maximum PSI.

Take out of the bag and roll flat

Check the spring nut

Attach the hose

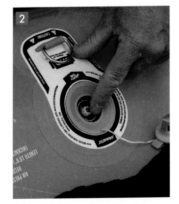
Pump up the board

Until full of air

Finish off at high pressure

The maximum pressure will be indicated either on your board or in the instruction manual. On an average board size of 10ft/4in to 10ft/6in, it will be 15-20PSI. The harder the board feels, the stiffer the ride and the more stable it will be. It's always worth pumping your ISUP to maximum pressure to get the most out of the board.

Inflatable boards can be left inflated for some time (hours, days or weeks) but they should not be left in direct sunlight, so semi-deflate them in hot climates and keep them out of the sun. Each time you go out on the water, check the pressure and top up with air if required.

You can buy double- or triple-chamber hand pumps or there are electric options (mains or car battery-powered, or rechargeable) to make it easier to get the maximum PSI out of your board. If you purchase an electric pump, check it is supplied with ISUP valve fitting for the hose. You can also buy high-pressure pump attachments, which make it easier to get to maximum PSI.

DEFLATING

When you come to deflate, remove the centre fin first if it's a removable fin, then undo the valve cover and push down the spring valve nut and turn it to the left or right. This will lock the nut down and you will hear a loud hiss of air. Once most of the air has escaped, roll the board from the nose to tail, squeezing out the last of the air inside. Then return the valve back to its inflate position and replace the valve cover. Now your board is ready to go back in the bag.

TROUBLESHOOTING

If your board deflates slowly from new, check the inflation valve is seated correctly in the board and tighten it up with a valve key to prevent air leaks.

Remove the fin

Take off the valve cover

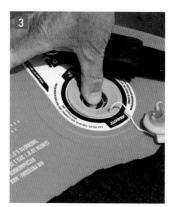
Depress the valve

Remove the air

Roll tightly

Put in the bag

WHERE TO RIDE

When you are starting out there is a big choice of water locations but not all are suitable. You need to be safe and understand tidal, wind and water conditions and water flow in rivers. These will affect the decision on where is good to ride.

Checking in with your local school / shop or SUP club will be the best way to start this process: they can give local advice, safety tips and, best of all, you can join in with them to build up your knowledge.

Inland your choices are from lakes, reservoirs, canals and rivers. Some of these are public, others private – so you may need permits or a licence. There are some great locations for SUP but there are some safety considerations like exit points, river flow, hazards, seasonal effects of wildlife, other water users, water quality and water temperatures. Remember, in the UK, the RNLI and Coastguard do not cover the inland waterways.

On rivers or canals: here on Chichester Canal

On a reservoir: here at Datchet Water with Windsor Castle in the background

For **coastal** paddleboarding, the weather, wind conditions and tides determine what is safe. Get some local advice on the best SUP conditions. Estuaries are popular for SUP as you get the feel of the ocean without being fully exposed to the open sea conditions.

On the **open coast** there are lots of good spots, but weather, tide and currents play a decisive role on how suitable these are for SUP. Pick your tide times to suit the location. Best is either slack or high tide and avoid the third and fourth hours in the tide cycle as this is when the current is strongest. Always think about wind speed and direction.

To find out best local places to SUP, try SUP schools and clubs, your local SUP shops and SUP magazines.

Estuaries are ideal for SUP: here Chichester Harbour

On the coast: here off West Wittering Beach in the UK

On the coast: here in Maui, Hawaii

WEATHER & SAFETY

CHECK THE WEATHER

Weather is a big subject, but the internet has brought all of this information directly to your computer or phone. The key to success on your SUP is how you interpret this information relative to your location.

Perfect conditions for SUP are as little wind as possible – onshore in direction (so you get blown back to land) and no moving water (tide /current / water flow). The top paddleboard speed for a beginner is somewhere between 2-3 knots. So, if the water is moving faster than that, you are not going to be able to paddle against it.

Before you head towards your chosen location, check at least two weather forecasts: try to use more specialist wind / weather forecasts such as windy.com, xcweather.co.uk, windguru.com, bigsalty.co.uk. These will give you an idea of what should be happening on the day.

When you arrive at your chosen SUP location the forecast may have been wrong or the weather may have changed. If you see dark black clouds and the wind direction has shifted, be aware.

There is an old-school way of reading wind and water called The Beaufort Scale which is still very relevant if you are heading out on the water (see opposite) – you are looking for force 0-3: calm to gentle breeze.

LOCATION

Choose a spot with little or no moving water (i.e. no tide or current), a place that is sheltered and you can access and exit the location in numerous places. Best practice would be to start by going with your SUP school or club to understand the location first before venturing off on your own. There is also no need to paddle out too far from the shore line: 30-50 metres max. For some locations you need a permit / to pay a launch fee and some you can ride for free, so it's worth checking before venturing out on the water.

SAFETY CHECK LIST

- Check the weather forecast
- Check the tide / water flow
- Stay within your physical and weather limits (light onshore winds, no water flow; avoid offshore winds)
- Always go with a friend and tell someone where you are going and what time you will be returning
- Wear a leash and buoyancy aid
- Wear the correct water wear for the season
- Take a safety bag and keep it on you (phone, first aid kit, drinking water, safety knife, spare leash, snacks, map of location)
- Keep close to shoreline (30-50 metres)
- Get local advice in new locations

INFORMATION

- RNLI: www.rnli.org/safety/choose-your-activity/stand-up-paddle-boarding
- Tide Times: www.ukho.gov.uk/easytide

Check the weather: you are looking for light winds

Beaufort No (Force)	Wind speed (knots)	General description	On land	On water	Suitability for SUP
0	0-1	Calm	Calm; smoke rises vertically	Water like a mirror	Ideal
1	1-3	Light air	Direction of wind shown by smoke drift but not wind vanes	Ripples	Ideal
2	4-6	Light breeze	Wind felt on face; leaves rustle	Small wavelets	Good
3	7-10	Gentle breeze	Leaves and small twigs in constant motion; wind extends light flags	Large wavelets; crests begin to break	Good
4	11-16	Moderate breeze	Raises dust and loose paper; small branches are moved	Small waves, becoming longer, fairly frequent white horses	If experienced
5	17-21	Fresh breeze	Small trees in leaf begin to sway	Moderate waves, many white horses, chance of some spray	Too windy
6	22-27	Strong breeze	Large branches in motion; umbrellas used with difficulty	Large waves begin to form; white foam crests are more extensive everywhere; probably some spray	Too windy
7	28-33	Near gale	Whole trees in motion	Sea heaps up & white foam from breaking waves begins to be blown in streaks	Too windy

TOURING

Touring, exploring, travelling over a distance on your SUP is an amazing part of the sport. Once you have mastered the basic techniques, got the right gear and safety plan, it opens up so many locations and travelling by water is not only relaxing, it is good for fitness, fun and sociable if you go with a group of friends.

Maybe on your first tour take a BSUPA lesson 'Ready to Tour' or go with a club to get all the information you need; but, if you are planning a tour, here is some advice before you head off.

Always check the weather forecast; understand the wind speed and direction and avoid offshore winds. You are still looking for light winds under 10 knots. If you are on the coast, check the tides or, if you are on a river, the river flow. Look for slack tide and low river flows. Take a map and identify the exit points on your planned route.

Keep your first tour short in distance, 2-4 kilometres, so you can determine your fitness level. It makes sense to stay within 30-50 metres from the shoreline.

It is worth taking a waterproof bag with a few pieces of safety gear inside: first aid bag, telephone, safety knife, map, some water, snacks and spare rope. Keep the bag on you not on your board!

Being out on the water there is always some risk, so tell someone where you are going and when you return. Always go with a friend and wear correct water wear for the time of year. Wear a buoyancy aid and always use your leash.

Although there are some safety considerations every time you go out on the water, once you get this dialled-in, touring is so much fun. You can then start ramping up the distance.

You can use an all-rounder board for touring or there are specific touring boards which are longer, have more of a pointy front end and are higher in volume for better gliding. With paddle height you tend to stick to the same height – 6 inches taller than you – but keep to the short paddle stroke, as this is a low-energy stroke: good for long distances.

You can tour with your SUP in some amazing places: here Hintersee Lake, Bavaria, Germany

There is a diverse range of events at a regional, national and international level. Racing is a great way to meet loads of like-minded SUP enthusiasts, improve your skill level, fitness and have fun. If you are going to get serious about it, the gear is more expensive and you will need to put in the pre-season training!

Racing comes in lots of different classes and is either by board length or type and then it gets split into different formats.

There are inflatable series on one-design boards, fun classes, 12ft 6in (3.8m) and 14ft (4.2m) board categories. The events are divided up into age and gender categories and the formats vary from sprints, technical, distance races, open ocean and downwind events with boards up to 18ft (5.4m). There are also mass-participation events which might be going from one place to another.

Hybrid SUP events have sprung up like SUP, BIKE, RUN and other versions of this concept – you can even compete at SUP polo.

There are Team Club events, which each season culminate in a national championship. When you have competed in national events there is a World Tour series with events around the globe and national team world championships.

There is a SURF SUP series where you compete on points for the best wave ride and national title events, which can earn you a place in the World Championships.

BRITISH & INTERNATIONAL SERIES

- **GBSUP UK National Race Series**: www.gbsup.co.uk
- **BSUPA National Surf SUP Series**: www.bsupa.org.uk
- **SUP BIKE RUN**: www.supbikerun.co.uk
- **N1SCO Series**: www.n1sco.com
- **APP World Tour**: www.appworldtour.com
- **British Club Championships**: www.facebook.com/pages/category/Community/British-SUP-Club-Championships-403596133140968/
- **ISA SUP worlds**: www.isasurf.org/events/isa-world-supand-paddleboard-championship-wsuppc/
- **USA**: www.supconnect.com
- **World**: www.supracer.com
- **Austaila**: www.oceanpaddler.com

Sprints, APP tour

Ladies distance race, APP tour

SUP SURFING

SUP was pretty much born out of the surf in its current form in the mid-1980s in Hawaii; large surfboards were used in smaller surf with a single-bladed paddle. In Hawaii, even small surf is a pretty good size!

Surfing on your SUP is exciting: being driven along by a moving piece of water feels good and, when you connect your paddle and turns together, it gets really exhilarating.

You can start your journey into waves on an all-round SUP, but a wide-style or regular shape surf SUP is a better option. These boards tend to be multi-fin type – 3, 4 or 5 fin boxes – so you can set your board as a quad or tri fin / thruster. Paddles tend to be shorter, around head height.

There are SUP surf shapes from just over 7ft (2.1m) for a pro, and up to 11ft (3.3m). Mid-range sizes are the most popular: 8-10.6ft (2.4-3.2m) with wide-style boards ideal for new SUP surfers.

Surfing on any wave is not straightforward, you need to know how to paddle out, turn, choose a wave, ride it, avoid others and fall safely. You also have to manage rips, tidal flows, wind, wind direction and the size of the surf. I would highly recommend that you take a lesson on this, as there is a lot to take in to start with.

Personal fitness also plays a big part in SUP surfing so start off in small waves – waist-high or less. You don't want to find yourself out the back with no energy to get back in. Avoid crowded line ups at all costs, find an empty wave and always wear a leash!

You can prone / kneel paddle out or try it standing up. Always approach the wave at a slight angle so, if the wave hits your board, it knocks it back and away from you. Remember **WAVE – BODY – BOARD** (to avoid the board hitting you).

When you see a wave you want to catch, do a step back turn as the wave approaches, switch your feet into surf stance, get low and paddle hard to catch the wave. Lean slightly into the wave and lift off – you should now be riding your first wave!

British Ex-National Champion SUP Surfer, Holly Bassett, enjoying the surf

Paddle out to the surf

Catch the wave

Start the carve turn

Use the paddle for counter balance

Straighten up

Go down the wave again

FITNESS

Fitness is a bi-product of doing lots of SUP; if you make time to get out on the water on a regular basis you will feel fitter, improve your core stability and mentally get that buzz and relaxation that comes with being in the great outdoors!

It takes a little more effort heading out on the water rather than going to the gym but I think the rewards from being on the water are far greater! You need to think of SUP more like a water bicycle: paddling a route can replace a run or a bike ride. Your pace, fitness and ability will dictate the intensity of your work rate and weather and water conditions will create variations in the result.

There are specific fitness and yoga courses run on SUPs at BSUPA centres and other schools; racing and touring are also a great way to stay fit. Paddling out in surf and catching waves is also a good fitness activity.

When you think about it, the board acts as an unstable platform: your body is constantly adjusting itself to maintain balance, then you pull your board and body in a forward direction with the paddle – it will challenge your core strength, balance and aerobic fitness.

Aside from the physical benefits of SUP – your mind just shuts off work, forgets about everyday life issues and you get that mental release and relax – it's very addictive!

Fitness and yoga courses are mostly run in flat water – SUP docking stations are popular – it means that instead of being inside a gym / studio, the great outdoors gives a different perspective to the class.

The extra balance that an SUP requires adds to the benefits of the class and provides an extra challenge to the session.

SUP has grown over recent years and you can book holidays at home or abroad with either a rental board and paddle options or a full-blown adventure trip paddleboarding every day in different locations with a guide, luxury accommodation and all the gear.

There are options for touring, fitness, yoga retreats, surf and race camps or just family trips with watersports companies who have SUP within the range of sports they offer.

The other option is taking your gear yourself. If it is by car or van, there are plenty of SUP locations both at home and not so far away.

Some companies offer accommodation and SUP use, others just offer rental or take your own gear and plan your own adventure.

You can travel on holiday with inflatable SUPs pretty easily. With 3-part paddles, the roller bags make this an easy project and open up loads of destinations for travel.

You can take rigid boards on airlines, but these are restricted to smaller sizes and you can have problems with damage. Check the airline's oversized baggage policy before booking. When you pack your board, put it into a padded travel bag and undo the air vent before flying.

Holidays on a SUP: here on Hintersee Lake, Bavaria, Germany

MAINTENANCE & REPAIR

MAINTENANCE

Keeping your SUP gear in good shape makes sense as, on the water, kit failure not only ruins a session but can have safety implications too!

Wash your board, paddle and wetsuit in freshwater each time you finish a session. Check the adjustable paddle handle is thoroughly washed to prevent jamming and wash wetsuits with a Milton's type product to prevent bacteria building up.

- Check the screws on your adjustable paddle handle: they sometimes loosen and may need a little tightening up.
- Every couple of months or so, scrub the deck pad down to remove any grease, oil, sunscreen and to retain its grip.
- Store your gear out of direct sunlight. Ultra-violet damage can age kit very quickly.
- Think about storage: suits on hangers, boards and paddle on a rack and stored somewhere dry.
- Check the fins: if the edges get rough or sharp, sand the sharp edges off.
- Check the leash for nicks or splits and replace if required.
- On inflatable boards the air valves need to be tightened up occasionally: use the valve key that is supplied and tighten the valve when required.

REPAIRS

Damage happens: if it is a small hole, split, crack or leak you may be able to fix it yourself; but for anything major I would suggest checking back with where you bought it, your local shop or SUP school to get the correct technical information to repair it. There are also specialist board / paddle and wetsuit repair centres.

INFLATABLE BOARD LEAKS

First always check the valve – this is the No.1 air leakage area and often a half turn with a valve key sorts out the problem.

If not, then you need to cover the board in water like a puncture repair on a bike inner tube and look for bubbles. Once you have found the spot: mark it, sand it and, when dry, glue a patch on (as per the manufacturer's instructions). Then either clamp or apply pressure to the patch and leave it for 24-48 hours to fix. Most inflatables are supplied with a repair kit, valve key, glue, patches and instructions. Any bigger holes or seam splits will need a specialist repairer.

ISUP repair: sandpaper the hole

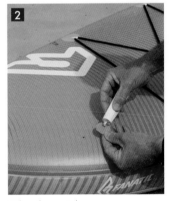

Glue the patch

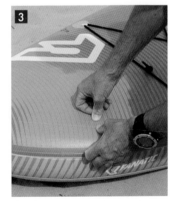

Apply pressure to the patch

Kit to repair a rigid board: gaffer tape, super glue, ding stick quick-repair putty, epoxy adhesive

EPOXY REPAIRS

The majority of rigid SUPs are made with epoxy resin but check the manufacturer's technical specifications first. If you get a small hole or crack, you need to stop using the board straight away and keep it out of the water. Dry the board out in a warm room and make certain the damaged area is dry.

A short-term gaffer tape repair

A short-term repair with super glue

As a short-term fix you could use Gaffer Tape and smooth this over a small hole. Super glue is another quick-fix: tape round the hole with masking tape and cover the crack / hole with glue to make it airtight.

There are also two-pack epoxy and ding stick epoxy quick-repair materials that can seal the damaged areas up and get you back on the water – these will often dry in minutes in warm temperatures.

If you are going to fix your board, read the manufacturer's instructions on both your board and the repair material. Work in a well-ventilated room and use some rubber gloves. Prepare the hole with some light sanding to remove jagged edges and mask around the hole before you repair it.

To get an 'as new' repair, find a local board repair shop – they are more costly, but also quicker and the board will look as new when finished!

Paddle repairs are trickier as there is more stress on this piece of gear so I would go to a repair shop for this.

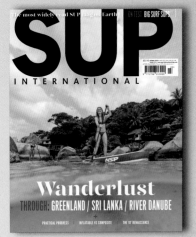

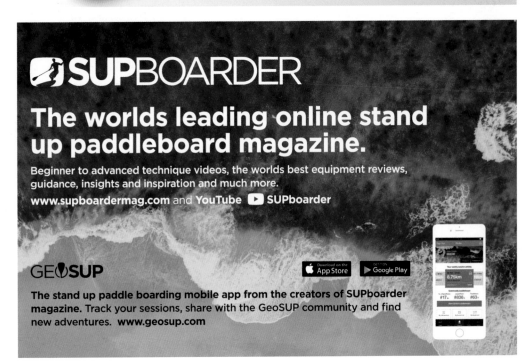

BSUPA
.ORG.UK

BRITISH STAND UP PADDLE ASSOCIATION

MEMBERSHIP | INSTRUCTORS | SCHOOLS | SAFETY

www.bsupa.org.uk

FERNHURST

B O O K S

We hope you enjoyed this book

If you did, **please post a review on Amazon**

Discover more books on

SAILING · RACING · CRUISING · MOTOR BOATING

SWIMMING · DIVING · SURFING

CANOEING · KAYAKING · FISHING

View our full range of titles at **www.fernhurstbooks.com**

Sign up to receive details of new books & exclusive special offers at

www.fernhurstbooks.com/register

Get to know us more on **social media**